The Baby Book Journal

The Baby Book Journal

BESTSELLING AUTHOR OF The Baby BOOK

RACHEL WADDILOVE

Text based on *The Baby Book* copyright © 2006, 2016 Rachel Waddilove
Illustrations copyright © 2016 Emma Skerratt, www.emmaskerratt.co.uk
Illustrations on pp. 31, 32, and 81 copyright © 2016 Kathy Wyatt, www.kathywyatt.com

This edition copyright © 2016 Lion Hudson

Published by Lion Books
an imprint of
Lion Hudson plc
Wilkinson House, Jordan Hill Road,
Oxford OX2 8DR, England
www.lionhudson.com/lion

ISBN 978 0 7459 6888 9

First edition 2016

Acknowledgments
Cover art © Emma Skerratt

A catalogue record for this book is available from the British Library

Printed and bound in China, September 2016, LH06

I dedicate this book to my darling children and grandchildren, who mean so much to me. I would not have been able to write it without them. To my son Ben, his wife Helen, and their children Hannah and Jessica; my daughter Sarah, her husband Reuben, and their children Zack, Bethany, and Joshua; and my daughter Jayne and her husband Peter: thank you for all your encouragement.

CONTENTS

INTRODUCTION

It is a very scary thing to come home from hospital with a newborn baby, whether you've had no experience of babies before or whether this is your third or fourth child. Often those first few days, and maybe weeks, after coming home from hospital can be very tearful times, particularly with the lack of sleep and perhaps the feeling of not quite knowing what to do. You may wonder how you are going to cope with this little bundle of life who seems to want continual feeding, particularly at the times when you just want to sleep.

My aim in writing *The Baby Book* has been to guide parents through the first year of their child's life. Many of my families have said to me over the years, 'It's time we had some good, sensible, down-to-earth, workable advice given to us to guide us in bringing up our families.' Society today has changed so much that we seldom have our parents and wider families around to encourage and help us with our newborn baby. My hope is that you will use this journal to write *your* personal story about your baby. Use these pages to help you plan your day and remember the essentials, jot down your thoughts and feelings, and create a journal full of beautiful memories to look back on. Enjoy!

Rachel x

1.

WELCOME

— To The —

WORLD

The TIME

The PLACE

Notes . . . ♥

DATE OF BIRTH

....

TIME OF BIRTH

....

DAY OF BIRTH

....

PLACE OF BIRTH

....

VITAL Statistics

WEIGHT:

LENGTH:

HAIR COLOUR:

EYE COLOUR:

AT BIRTH YOU LOOKED LIKE...

I/WE

NAME

YOU

FIRST NAME

....

MIDDLE NAME(S)

....

WE CHOSE THESE NAMES BECAUSE

....

....

Because YOU CAN NEVER HAVE Too Many PHOTOS

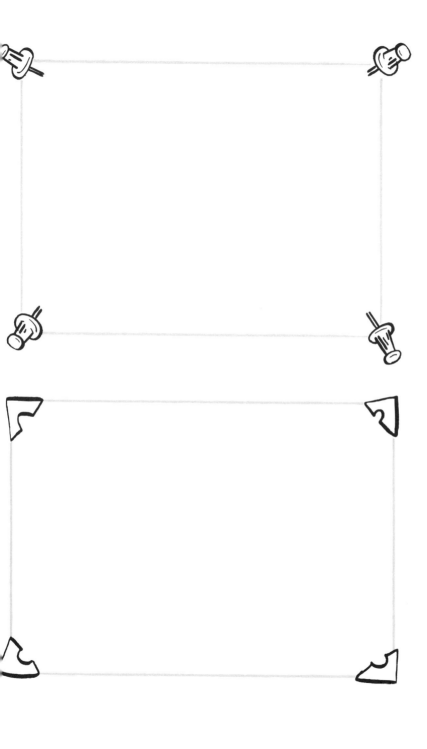

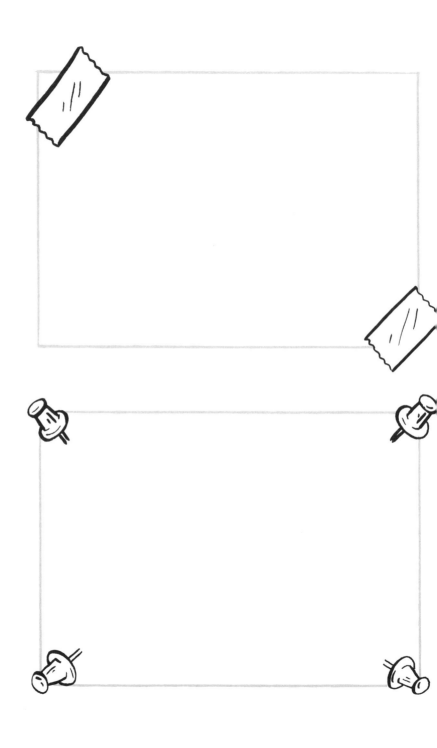

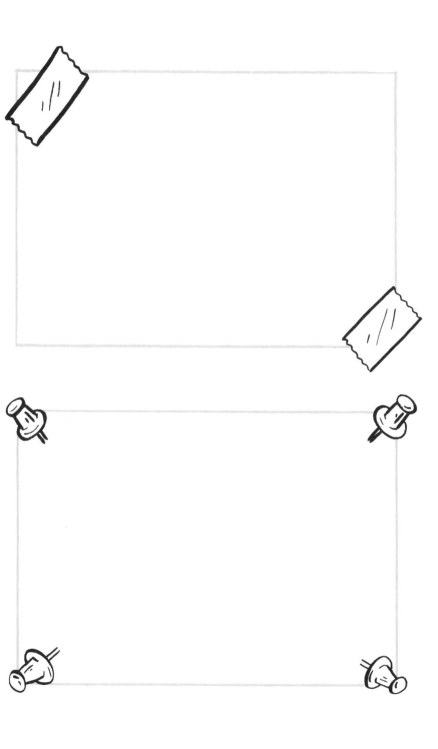

2.

PREPARING FOR MY

BABY

A WORD FROM Rachel...

As you begin to prepare for the
birth of your baby, you may find
that you start making lists of all the
things that you will need to buy,
borrow and acquire!
The next few pages offer you a place
to plan what you will need for your
stay in hospital and the first few
months of your baby's life.

———   ♥   ———

WHAT I NEED FOR LABOUR

- ☐ antenatal notes
- ☐ birth plan (if I've made one)
- ☐ tens machine (if using one)
- ☐ nightdress / large shirt for delivery
- ☐ thick socks
- ☐ snacks and drinks

- ☐ magazines and books
- ☐ dressing gown and slippers
- ☐ camera
- ☐ lip balm and facial spray
- ☐ wash bag and hairbrush / bands
- ☐
- ☐
- ☐

WHAT I NEED FOR HOSPITAL

- ☐ two or three nightdresses or pyjamas (front-opening for feeding)
- ☐ three nursing bras
- ☐ breast pads
- ☐ nipple cream
- ☐ disposable or cheap underpants
- ☐ at least twenty-four maternity pads
- ☐ two towels
- ☐ tissues
- ☐ make-up bag
- ☐ arnica tablets / cream
- ☐ antibacterial wipes
- ☐ mobile phone and charger
- ☐ clothes for going home (maternity wear)
- ☐ _____
- ☐ _____

WHAT I NEED FOR MY BABY

- newborn nappies
- three vests
- three sleepsuits
- muslin squares
- shawl or blanket
- clothes for going home
- warm jacket or all-in-one if cold weather
-
-
-

Things my BABY NEEDS

- [ ]
- [ ]
- [ ]
- [ ]

NEWBORN ESSENTIALS

- at least six short-sleeved vests / bodysuits with poppers between the legs
- at least six sleepsuits (babygrows)
- two or three cardigans
- one all-in-one or warm jacket for going outside in winter
- at least two hats
- at least two pairs of bootees or socks
- mittens (optional)
- bibs

SLEEP ESSENTIALS

························

- ❑ Moses basket / crib and mattress
- ❑ drop-side cot and mattress
- ❑ bedding for the Moses basket: at least four fitted sheets
- ❑ four cellular cotton blankets
- ❑ four flat sheets (optional)
- ❑ bedding for the drop-side cot:
  - ★ four fitted sheets
  - ★ four flat sheets (optional)
  - ★ four large blankets
  - ★ twelve to twenty-four muslin squares (place under your baby's head to catch any milk he brings up)
- ❑ two shawls for swaddling or four large muslins
- ❑ room temperature gauge (optional)
- ❑ baby monitor

BREASTFEEDING ESSENTIALS

- ☐ plenty of breast pads
- ☐ at least two nursing bras
- ☐ nipple cream
- ☐ breast pump, hand or electric
- ☐ freezer bags for freezing breast milk
- ☐ 2 x 100 ml (4 fl oz) bottles
- ☐ size 1 newborn teats
- ☐ bottle sterilizer
- ☐ nursing chair (optional)
- ☐ nursing pillow
  (not essential; ordinary pillows
  are just as good)
- ☐ small boxes of ready-
  made formula
  (optional)

BOTTLE FEEDING ESSENTIALS

- [ ] 2 x 100 ml (4 fl oz) bottles with teats
- [ ] 6 x 200 ml (8 fl oz) bottles with teats
- [ ] size 1 newborn teats
- [ ] bottle sterilizer
- [ ] plastic jug for warming bottles
- [ ] box of formula suitable for newborns
- [ ] bottle brush
- [ ] electric bottle warmer (optional)
- [ ] milk powder dispenser (optional)

CHANGING ESSENTIALS

- ❑ changing mat
- ❑ changing unit with safety strap (optional)
- ❑ cotton wool
- ❑ newborn nappies (disposable or washable)
- ❑ barrier cream for your baby's bottom
- ❑ baby wipes (use from two weeks onwards)
- ❑ nappy bin or nappy wrapper
- ❑ disposable changing mat liners (optional)

BATHING ESSENTIALS

- ☐ two bath towels or baby towels with hoods
- ☐ two hand towels
- ☐ two sponges (optional)
- ☐ two soft flannels
- ☐ baby soap or liquid wash
- ☐ cotton wool
- ☐ moisturizing cream or lotion
- ☐ baby oil (olive oil is just as good)
- ☐ shampoo
- ☐ a soft hairbrush
- ☐ baby nail scissors with rounded tips
- ☐ bath thermometer (optional)
- ☐ waterproof bathing apron (optional but very useful)
- ☐ baby bath and stand (optional)

TRAVEL ESSENTIALS

- ☐ rear-facing car seat suitable from birth
- ☐ pram and / or pushchair / travel system suitable from birth
- ☐ changing bag
- ☐ baby sling or carrier (optional)
- ☐ travel cot (optional)

PLAYTIME

- ☐ black and white baby books / toys
- ☐ soft toys suitable from birth
- ☐ adjustable or bouncy chair
- ☐ activity gym
- ☐ activity arch for car seat / bouncy chair
- ☐ musical toys / mobile

'As long as he has something to wear, clean nappies, somewhere to sleep, and plenty to eat, he will be perfectly happy.'

THINGS I have BEEN GIVEN

Gifts for my BABY

GIFT	FROM	THANK YO

GIFT	FROM	THANK YOU

3.

Coming

HOME

FROM

Hospital

Over the years many parents have told me
that they were well-prepared for pregnancy
and birth, but not for how they would
actually feel when they got home.
Often, professionals assume that parents will
find it difficult to take in lots of information
about coping with life after the birth.
However, in my experience parents wish that
they had been better informed and had time
to prepare for the emotional ups and downs
of life with a new baby.

•   •   •   •   •   ♥   •   •   •   •   •

HOW I'M FEELING

MIND

BODY

SOUL

MIND
....

bonding

WORRY

tiredness

mood swings

BONDING

A great emphasis has been placed on bonding with your baby in recent years, and many parents worry about whether this will happen immediately. Most parents feel a huge rush of love when they see their baby for the first time, and birth really is an amazing experience.

However, not every parent feels this overwhelming sense of love when they first see their baby. Don't worry if this happens to you, as bonding is simply about the baby and parents getting to know each other, and your love for your baby will deepen over a period of time.

'Try to be as relaxed with your baby as possible, giving him lots of cuddles and unconditional love.'

Write down your precious bonding moments here:

WORRY

We don't have the luxury of a practice run at parenting, and both you and your partner may worry that you are not going to be a good mum or dad. It is important to try to feel happy with yourself, as there really is no such thing as the perfect parent.

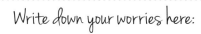

Write down your worries here:

MOOD SWINGS

→ Observe any mood swings, along with notes about the time of day, what you have eaten, and when you last slept!

'Mood swings are quite normal, especially if you're breastfeeding.'

MEMORY LOSS

Memory loss is often due to hormonal changes in your body and sleep deprivation. Your memory will come back, but give yourself a bit of time, as your body has been going through huge changes over the last nine months.

A SPACE TO WRITE DOWN IMPORTANT THINGS TO REMEMBER:

TIREDNESS

There will be days when you feel really exhausted, especially as you will be having broken nights. At this stage, the best thing you can do for yourself and the baby is to rest whenever you have the opportunity. Don't worry if you need to sleep when your baby is sleeping. If you can, hold on to the fact that the extreme tiredness will pass as your baby gets bigger and sleeps for longer at night.

I FEEL TIRED WHEN

THESE THINGS HELP ME TO FEEL LESS TIRED

REST

· · · · · · · ·

RACHEL'S TOP TIPS FOR GETTING REST

1. Don't feel the need to rush anything. Take time to really enjoy your baby, remember that becoming a parent is a wonderful experience even through the ups and downs.

2. A flexible routine helps your baby to feed well and sleep well, and for you to rest well.

3. Rest when your baby sleeps – the housework can wait!

4. During the daytime, feed your baby on your bed so that you can rest while feeding.

5. Take every opportunity to put your feet up!

'Rest for six weeks, eat well, and you won't look back.'

NUTRITION

· · · · · · · · · · · · · · · ·

*'You need an extra
600 calories per
day if you are
breastfeeding.'*

Have a good, balanced diet and aim to have at
least one cooked meal during the day, as well
as having healthy snacks while feeding. It's
important to make sure that your fluid intake
is good, as this will also help increase your milk
supply. Have plenty to drink, including water,
juices, or hot drinks – whatever you like.

Food that gives me energy

Food that I enjoy

LOOKING AFTER MY BODY

It's perfectly normal to have some bruising and soreness after giving birth. Having plenty of hot baths with a few drops of lavender oil can help to soothe and heal the perineal area.

However, remember that it took nine months for your body to grow and develop while carrying your baby, so don't expect it to return to normal that quickly. Allow your body time to heal and recover.

EXERCISE

It is a good idea to have a little walk each day if you feel like it, but don't overdo it. Often, just getting outside in the fresh air even for half an hour will do you good. Even in the winter, it's worth wrapping up and going out for a walk, as it can really give you a lift. Gentle exercise will help you regain your figure, but don't do any strenuous exercise until after your postnatal check-up.

EXERCISES I CAN DO	EXERCISES I LIKE TO DO!

ME TIME

A treat for me is...

> 'Try to treat yourself to something you really enjoy when you feel like going out again, perhaps going to the hairdresser or having a massage.'

··············

> 'My message to dads is that they
> need to get rest when they can and
> not to be too hard on themselves.'

What my partner needs...

_____

_____

_____

_____

_____

_____

_____

_____

_____

_____

_____

Write down here your ideas for doing
things together as a couple:

MONDAY	TUESDAY	WEDNESDAY	THURSDAY

FRIDAY	SATURDAY	SUNDAY
date night		

Notes . . . ♥

COPING WITH DIFFICULT
CIRCUMSTANCES

'Try to organize some help
before you have your baby, so
that somebody is on hand for
you when you come home.
It is important to have as much
support and help as possible
when you're going through a
difficult time as well as looking
after a newborn baby.'

SUPPORT FROM OTHERS

How people have helped me when I needed them:

SOUL

Time to reflect

Meditation

Blessings

PRAYER

REFLECT

. . . .

How I am blessed…

PRAYER / MEDITATION

4.

MY BIRTH

STORY

You may find it helpful to write your birth experience down, particularly if it was not what you had expected or planned for. After I had our babies I wrote my birth story, describing my feelings and the whole experience, and I'm sure this was a help to me in the early weeks.

MY BIRTH STORY

· ·

The GOOD bits
I choose to
REMEMBER!

If I choose to have
ANOTHER
BABY,
will REMEMBER this...

what I am
GRATEFUL for about my
BIRTH EXPERIENCE

5.

The DAY

TO

DAY with my

BABY

FEEDING

Most parents feel overwhelmed by the responsibility of caring for a newborn baby when they first come home from hospital. This is perfectly normal, and you will find that your initial fear passes as you get to know your baby and become confident in how to look after him. The following pages will give you helpful lists and guidelines to follow and to add to about the practical aspects of baby care, particularly if this is your first child and you haven't had much experience of babies.

THE ENVIRONMENT FOR FEEDING

It's important for both you and your baby
to be comfortable when feeding.
Before you begin to feed, wash your hands
and have everything to hand that you'll
need for feed time.

- a jug of water and a glass
  (you need to drink plenty if breastfeeding)
- snacks
- a bottle and warmer, if bottle feeding or using
  expressed milk
- a changing mat
- a clean nappy
- cotton wool and a small bowl of warm water
- a nappy sack
- nappy rash cream (only necessary if his
  bottom is sore)
- clean breast pads if needed
- a muslin for any milk brought up
- a pillow or specialist feeding pillow

BASIC FEEDING POSITION

There are three main positions for breastfeeding. The basic one is for you to sit up and hold your baby in your arms with his head cradled in the crook of your arm and his tummy facing you. It often helps to put a pillow on your lap under your baby's body to bring him up to your breast, so that you don't have to lean over him. You may find that you get bad headaches if you regularly lean over when feeding. It's important to keep his body tucked closely into yours, and you can put your hand on his back to help support him. The other hand is then free to put your breast to him. He will usually turn his head towards your breast (this is called rooting), and this is the right position for him to latch on. A nice way to remember this position is 'nose to nipple and tummy to mummy'.

my FEEDING Journal

DATE

TIME AWAKE	FEED (START TIME)	BOTTLE OR BREAST (R/L)	BOTTLE:ML BREAST:DURATION	LENGTH OF TIME AWAKE	TIME SETTLED FOR SLEEP

NOTES

Keeping a feeding journal can help you to get to know your baby's feeding habits, and guide you in establishing a routine.

DATE

TIME AWAKE	FEED (START TIME)	BOTTLE OR BREAST (R/L)	BOTTLE:ML BREAST:DURATION	LENGTH OF TIME AWAKE	TIME SETTLED FOR SLEEP

NOTES

my FEEDING Journal

DATE

TIME AWAKE	FEED (START TIME)	BOTTLE OR BREAST (R/L)	BOTTLE:ML BREAST:DURATION	LENGTH OF TIME AWAKE	TIME SETTLED FOR SLEEP

NOTES

my FEEDING Journal

DATE

TIME AWAKE	FEED (START TIME)	BOTTLE OR BREAST (R/L)	BOTTLE:ML BREAST:DURATION	LENGTH OF TIME AWAKE	TIME SETTLED FOR SLEEP

NOTES

ESTABLISHING

a flexible

ROUTINE

On the following pages are some of my suggestions for establishing a routine in feed and sleep times for babies from newborn to twelve months. This approach helps you to teach your baby structure in her day, and enables you to know when feed times are so that you can have structure in your day too.

. . . .
. . . .

THREE-HOURLY FEEDING ROUTINE

KEY

FEED BABY

BATH BABY

PUT BABY TO SLEEP

9.00 TO 10.00 A.M.

- ✳ Wake your baby up if he's not already awake.
- ✳ Feed and wind your baby.
- ✳ Top and tail.
- ✳ Dress your baby in day clothes.
- ✳ Spend a little time cuddling and talking to your baby.
- ✳ Change nappy if dirty.

10.00 TO 11.00 A.M.

- ✳ Swaddle your baby.
- ✳ Put your baby in her cot or pram for a morning sleep.
- ✳ Your baby will probably sleep until about 12.00 noon.
- ✳ Don't forget to make yourself a cuppa and have a sit down while your baby is sleeping!

12.00 TO 1.00 P.M.

* Wake your baby if he's asleep.
* Feed and wind your baby.
* Change your baby's nappy either before or halfway through the feed if you need to wake him up and encourage him to take a good feed.
* Spend a little time cuddling and talking to your baby.
* Change nappy if you haven't changed it during feed.

 1.00 TO 2.00 P.M.

* Swaddle your baby and tuck down in cot or pram.
* You can take your baby out for a walk in the pram or buggy if you are not too tired.
* Your baby will probably sleep until about 3.00 p.m.
* Don't forget to grab some lunch and put your feet up while your baby sleeps.

 3.00 TO 4.00 P.M.

* Wake your baby if she's asleep.
* Feed and wind your baby.
* Change your baby's nappy if you haven't changed it during feed.
* Cuddle time.

 4.00 TO 5.00 P.M.

* Swaddle your baby and tuck down in cot or pram.
* You can take your baby out for a walk in the pram or buggy if you are not too tired.
* Your baby will probably sleep until about 5.30 p.m.

 **BATHTIME, 5.30 TO 6.00 P.M.**

- ⋆ Bathtime.
- ⋆ Dress your baby in night clothes.
- ⋆ Use this time for cuddles and talking to your baby.

 6.00 TO 7.00 P.M.

- ⋆ Spend this time quietly with your baby, as after this feed you will settle him for the evening in her cot.
- ⋆ Feed and wind baby.
- ⋆ Only change nappy if dirty.

 BEDTIME, 7.00 TO 8.00 P.M.

- ⋆ Ensure your baby has had a good feed.
- ⋆ Ensure your baby has brought up all his wind.
- ⋆ Swaddle and tuck your baby into cot; this is the beginning of teaching her that this is night and not day.
- ⋆ Your baby may sleep until around 9.00 to 10.00 p.m.

 DREAM FEED, 9.00 TO 11.00 P.M.

- ⋆ If your baby is asleep, wake him by 11.00 p.m.
- ⋆ Feed him.
- ⋆ Spend time over this feed, sitting quietly with your baby.
- ⋆ Change nappy and wind halfway through feed.
- ⋆ Finish feed.
- ⋆ Swaddle and tuck into cot by 12.00 midnight.

OPTIONAL EXTRA NIGHT FEED, 12.00 TO 1.00 A.M.

* Feed when your baby wakes (or wake your baby if she is underweight or unwell).
* Change nappy only if dirty or if she's sleepy during feed.
* Wind your baby. Quietly tuck back into cot after feed.
* Your baby will probably sleep for around another 3-4 hours.

12.00 TO 4.00 A.M.

* Wait for your baby to wake naturally.
* Feed.
* Wind and change nappy.
* Quietly tuck back into cot after feed.
* Your baby will probably sleep until around 4.00 to 6.00 a.m.

4.00 TO 6.00 A.M.

* Wait for your baby to wake naturally.
* Feed.
* Wind and change nappy.
* Quietly tuck back into cot after feed.
* Try to take this opportunity to go back to sleep yourself until the next feed.

FOUR-HOURLY FEEDING

 ### 10.00 TO 11.00 A.M.

* Wake your baby up if he's not already awake.
* Top and tail.
* Dress your baby in day clothes.
* Begin feed by 11.00 a.m.
* Feed and wind baby.
* Spend time cuddling and talking to your baby.
* Change nappy if dirty.

 ### 11.00 A.M. TO 12.00 NOON

* Swaddle your baby.
* Put your baby in her cot or pram for a morning sleep.
* Your baby can be taken out for a walk in the pram or buggy.
* Your baby will probably sleep until about 2.00 p.m.

 ### 2.00 TO 3.00 P.M.

* Wake your baby if she's asleep.
* Feed.
* Change your baby's nappy either before or halfway through the feed, particularly if she's very sleepy, as this will help to wake her up and encourage her to feed again.
* Wind during nappy change.
* Finish feed.
* Spend time cuddling and talking to your baby.
* Change nappy if you haven't changed it during feed.

 **3.00 TO 4.00 P.M.**

* Swaddle your baby and tuck down in cot or pram.
* Your baby can be taken out for a walk in pram or buggy.
* Your baby will probably sleep until approximately 5.30 p.m.

 **BATHTIME, 5.30 TO 6.00 P.M.**

* Bathtime.
* Dress your baby in night clothes.
* Use this time for cuddles and talking to your baby.

 6.00 TO 7.00 P.M.

* Feed.
* Spend this time quietly with your baby, as after this feed you will settle him for the evening in his cot.
* Wind your baby.
* Only change nappy if dirty.

 BEDTIME, 7.00 TO 8.00 P.M.

* Ensure your baby has had a good feed.
* Ensure your baby has brought up all her wind.
* Swaddle and tuck your baby into cot; this is the beginning of teaching her that this is night and not day.
* Your baby may sleep until approximately 10.00 p.m.

DREAM FEED, 10.00 TO 11.30 P.M.

- ∗ If your baby is asleep, wake him by 11.30 p.m.
- ∗ Feed him.
- ∗ Spend time over this feed, sitting quietly with your baby.
- ∗ Change nappy and wind halfway through feed.
- ∗ Finish feed.
- ∗ Swaddle and tuck into cot by 12.00 midnight.

NIGHT FEED, 2.00 TO 4.00 A.M.

- ∗ Feed when your baby wakes naturally.
- ∗ Change nappy only if dirty or if she's sleepy during feed.
- ∗ Wind your baby.
- ∗ Quietly tuck back into cot after feed.
- ∗ Your baby will probably sleep for around four hours.

6.00 TO 7.00 A.M.

- ∗ Wake your baby by 7.00 a.m. if he's not woken before then.
- ∗ Feed.
- ∗ Wind and change nappy.
- ∗ Make time for cuddles and talking to your baby.
- ∗ If your baby is wakeful, he can be up for a little while.
- ∗ Do try to go back to bed after this feed if you can and rest until the 10.00-11.00 a.m. feed.

Notes...

Going FORWARD

By three to six months, your baby will probably
be well and truly settled into a four-hourly
feeding routine. The routine for three to six
months stays much the same, the only difference
being that you will drop another feed. This can
either be the 10.00–11.00 p.m. feed or the
7.00 a.m. feed. You may prefer to drop the
10.00–11.00 p.m. feed if you need to get up
for work or other commitments in the morning.
I've found that most families prefer to drop this
feed first. However, if you're a night owl you may
want to drop the 7.00 a.m. feed and keep the
10.00–11.00 p.m. feed, and this is fine.

BIRTH TO ONE MONTH (FOUR-HOURLY FEEDING)

10.00 to 11.00 a.m.

2.00 to 3.00 p.m.

6.00 to 7.00 p.m.

10.00 to 11.30 p.m. dream feed

2.00 to 4.00 a.m. night feed

6.00 to 7.00 a.m.

DAILY TIMINGS, ONE TO TWO MONTHS

10.00 to 11.00 a.m.

2.00 to 3.00 p.m.

(5.00 p.m. optional top-up feed)

6.00 to 7.00 p.m.

10.00 to 11.30 p.m. dream feed

2.00 to 4.00 a.m. optional night feed

6.00 to 7.00 a.m.

Babies who are taught to sleep early on
will be happy and contented and will
generally grow up to be good sleepers.
Parents also need sleep!
It is important to form good sleeping
habits in the first few months of life to
help your baby understand the difference
between night and day.
By six months of age, a baby with good
sleep habits should regularly sleep through
the night for at least twelve hours.

DAY	AMOUNT OF TIME SLEPT	NIGHT SLEEP	DAY SLEEP	MY OBSERVATIONS

DAY	AMOUNT OF TIME SLEPT	NIGHT SLEEP	DAY SLEEP	MY OBSERVATIONS

DAY	AMOUNT OF TIME SLEPT	NIGHT SLEEP	DAY SLEEP	MY OBSERVATIONS

CRYING

I find one of the things new parents worry about most is their baby crying and how they should deal with it. Anxiety about your baby crying is natural; however, it's good to remember that babies need to cry as they can't talk, so crying is an important part of their expression and development. A good cry doesn't harm your baby, and in the early days of life it can help to expand the lungs and is a sign of healthy development. In fact, if our babies didn't cry we would worry.

My baby cries when ....

introducing SOLID FOOD

There are two main reasons for starting solids:
to satisfy your baby's increasing appetitc, and to
introduce him to the pleasure of new tastes and
textures. My approach is to always recommend
starting your baby with purées.

These are gentle foods and as such are very easy
on a baby's tummy. Baby rice mixed with purées,
such as dessert apple, pears, apricots, or puréed
vegetables are very digestible as first-time foods.

EQUIPMENT I WILL NEED FOR FEEDING

- ★ plastic weaning spoons
- ★ plastic bowls or bottle-lids for small amounts of food
- ★ ice cube trays for freezing purées
- ★ plastic storage containers for food
- ★ bibs
- ★ bouncy chair for the first few months
- ★ highchair (for later)
- ★ plastic mat to protect floor under feeding chair (optional)
- ★ saucepan or steamer
- ★ blender
- ★ baby rice

what my BABY ATE and What S/HE Like

DATE:

FOOD EATEN:

BABY'S REACTION:
☺ 😐 ☹
☐ ☐ ☐

DATE:

FOOD EATEN:

BABY'S REACTION:
☺ 😐 ☹
☐ ☐ ☐

DATE:

FOOD EATEN:

BABY'S REACTION:
☺ 😐 ☹
☐ ☐ ☐

DATE:

FOOD EATEN:

BABY'S REACTION:
☺ 😐 ☹
☐ ☐ ☐

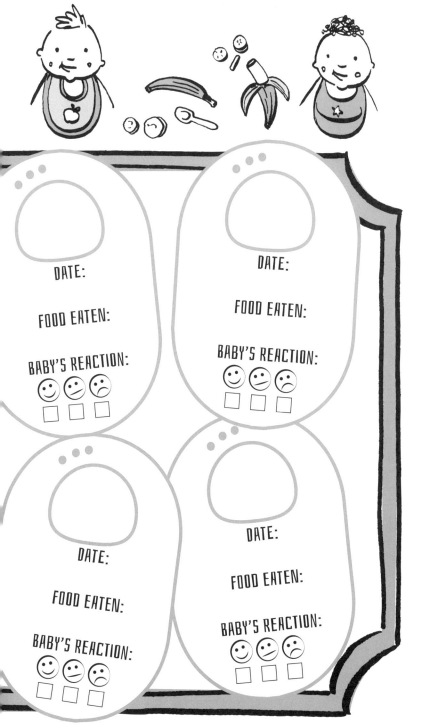

DATE:

FOOD EATEN:

BABY'S REACTION:

DATE:

FOOD EATEN:

BABY'S REACTION:

DATE:

FOOD EATEN:

BABY'S REACTION:

DATE:

FOOD EATEN:

BABY'S REACTION:

RECIPES

Write your recipes for your baby's favourite food here:

RECIPES

6.

♥ —— —— ♥

MY
BABY

♥ —— —— ♥

Doctor's checks

DATE	CHECK-UP	RESULTS

DATE	CHECK-UP	RESULTS

my BABY'S
immunizations & Dates

DATE	IMMUNIZATION	REACTION?

How my BABY has GROWN

DATE	WEIGHT	LENGTH

My BABY's SENSES

My baby likes to:

Smell...

Taste...

Look at...

LISTEN TO...

my BABY'S FIRSTS!

TOOTH

SMILE

STEPS

SWIM

FOOD

7.

OUR FAMILY

A WORD FROM *Rachel*...

Family life is the foundation of society everywhere in the world, producing enrichment and stability. It is a privilege as parents to develop and nurture a new generation, and to instil confidence in your child of her worth and value.

PEOPLE

in my

BABY'S

Life

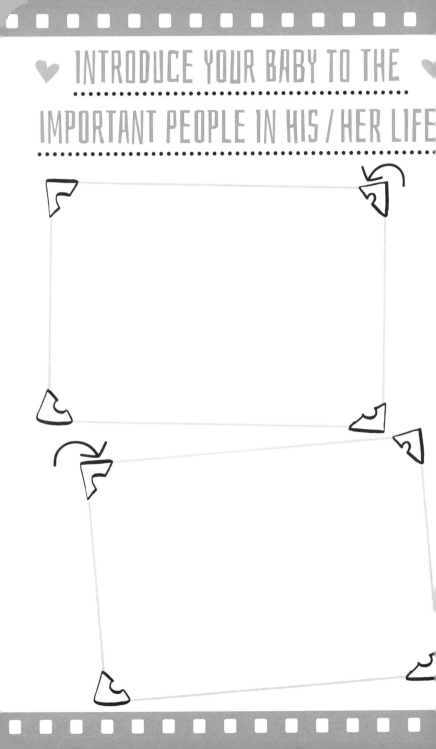

OUR FAMILY

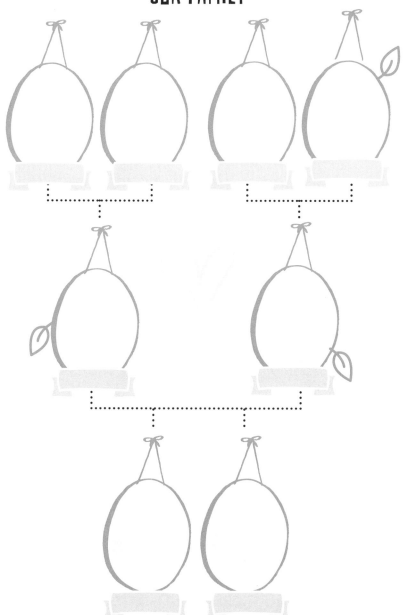

Because YOU CAN NEVER HAVE Too Many PHOTOS

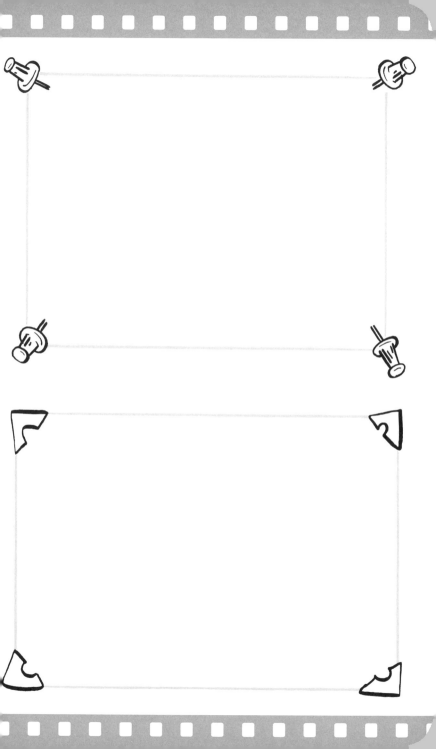

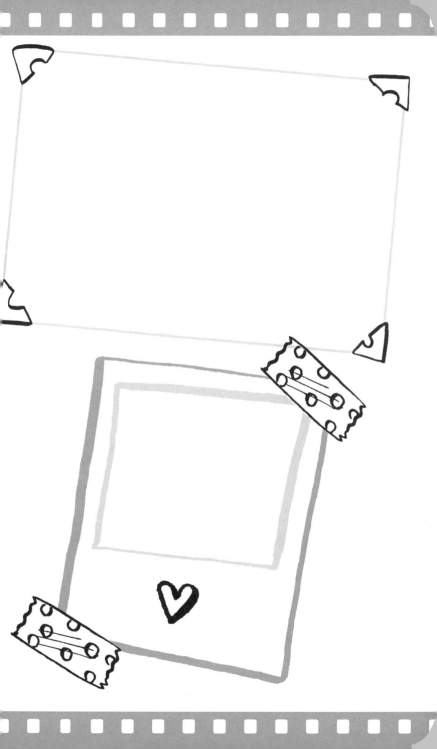

8.

the
SPIRITUAL
and
EMOTIONAL
NEEDS
of my
BABY

I personally believe that babies are not just body and mind, but have a spiritual side too. As parents, you instinctively care for your baby's physical needs, but you can also nurture his spiritual and emotional needs as he grows up.

For me, the nature and character of God is love, and there are many aspects of this love that we can share as families. I believe that God can equip us as parents with love, joy, peace, patience, kindness and gentleness, faithfulness, and self-control (found in Galatians 5:22–23).

Use these pages to record your precious memories...

Showing my
BABY LOVE

Sharing in the Joy

CELEBRATING
moments of
PEACE

Showing
— PATIENCE —

DEMONSTRATING
Kindness and goodness

Holding on to Faithfulness

Demonstrating,
SELF-CONTROL

A PRAYER

Write a prayer or blessing for your
baby here:

Reflecting on Hard Times

My thoughts and worries...

Reflecting on Beauty

Beautiful memories...

My *Journal*